West Portal

THE AGHA SHAHID ALI PRIZE IN POETRY

WEST PORTAL

BENJAMIN **GUCCIARDI**

FOREWORD BY GABRIELLE CALVOCORESSI

THE **UNIVERSITY OF UTAH PRESS**   SALT LAKE CITY

AGHA SHAHID ALI

PRIZE IN POETRY

THE AGHA SHAHID ALI PRIZE IN POETRY
Series Editor: Katharine Coles

The Defiance House Man colophon is a registered trademark of
The University of Utah Press. It is based on a four-foot-tall Ancient
Puebloan pictograph (late PIII) near Glen Canyon, Utah.

LIBRARY OF CONGRESS CATALOGING-IN-PUBLICATION DATA
Names: Gucciardi, Benjamin, 1984- author.
Title: West Portal / Benjamin Gucciardi.
Other titles: Agha Shahid Ali prize in poetry.
Description: Salt Lake City : The University of Utah Press, [2021] |
   Series: Agha Shahid Ali prize in poetry
Identifiers: LCCN 2020057466 (print) | LCCN 2020057467 (ebook) | ISBN
   9781647690403 (paperback) | ISBN 9781647690410 (ebook)
Subjects: LCSH: West Portal (San Francisco, Calif.)--Poetry. | LCGFT:
   Poetry.
Classification: LCC PS3607.U27 W47 2021 (print) | LCC PS3607.U27 (ebook)
   | DDC 811/.6--dc23
LC record available at https://lccn.loc.gov/2020057466
LC ebook record available at https://lccn.loc.gov/2020057467

Errata and further information on this and other titles available online at
UofUpress.com

Printed and bound in the United States of America.

Contents

Foreword

by Gabrielle Calvocoressi

It is not only trauma which cleaves—
the soul also fractures in joy.
—Benjamin Gucciardi, *from* "Hunting Chanterelles in the Oakland Hills"

I find Benjamin Gucciardi's book, West Portal to be really beautiful. That's not something I mean lightly and it's something I take seriously. Because so often beauty in poems simply resides on the surface, which makes them sort of like papier-mâché birds: lovely until I really come up close to them and then I just feel fooled and foolish. Plus, it's a moment in our history (public and private) that feels really devoid of beauty. And also, as so many are dying and being killed, it is a moment where I wonder if I even deserve beauty. If that's something I should be hoping for. Recently some students brought this up to me. They wondered if it was even ethical to think about things like beauty and pleasure right now. And I said, I felt searching out beauty and pleasure is often a radical act. Particularly because trouble and terror are waiting on the other side of everything. Particularly right now in the fall of 2020.

What's beautiful to me about Benjamin Gucciardi's poems is exactly this. The beautiful and the terrible live alongside each other in this work. And so often, they're actually the same thing. Or they are happening all at once. The speaker in these poems is a teacher, is a brother, is a human vessel whose health is precarious. There are ghosts everywhere, and everywhere in these poems people are being forced to make the best of terrible situations. Often these people are very young and the poet is also a teacher who is trying to make some kind of space of welcome and care when it is clear that there is no welcome that will keep these people safe.

Why do we keep trying? is a question this book seems to ask. Even the city this book largely takes place in, San Francisco, is its own kind of brutality. Predatory capitalism breaks everyone in one way or another. The rent is too high. There is nowhere to live. The egret stands amidst the rings of petrol. And yet. In every moment of loss there are kids hugging, lovers making a life together, the body goes to swim in the ocean even if the ocean itself is ailing. "What is a bruise but the body fighting back?" the poet asks us, and I am caught off guard by the feeling of hope that fills me in that moment. There is such deep searching in this book and such formal precision. And the language is luminous, which makes the harrowing physical and psychic landscape even more profound. At the center of this world is the ghost of the poet's sister, who proves that ghosts are always the best teachers. They see us. They're past caring. But also they open the space where we might learn to care more deeply both for ourselves and for others. What a gift it is to have a ghost visit one's book.

Yes. Benjamin Gucciardi has written a book that I keep coming back to and learning from. And I keep thinking, "this world of poems is really beautiful." Which is to say, it's also really terrible. I'm such a fan of how this book acknowledges that you can't have one without the other. I'll be reading this book for a really long time.

—October 9, 2020

West Portal (n):

A hushed, residential neighborhood in southwestern San Francisco at the base of Twin Peaks.

The western terminus of an underground passage; the point where a train emerges into a city's western quadrant, or the end of a tunnel dug beneath razor wire.

An entryway into the afterworld—the westward movement of the soul after the body dies, following the path of the setting sun.

1.

Type Two

Five times a day, I prick my finger
and ask my blood about its failure.

Out of its cage,
it wants to discuss its better cages:

How, before it was mine, it lived inside
a python near Varanasi—

the thrill of rushing
when muscle snaps a rabbit's spine.

How it wants to paint a self-portrait
as the Ganges river—

in the foreground, a woman in a yellow sari
cleanses her son's limp body, his skin

the color of the river, the river
the color of her eyes.

That's how holy I am,
it says, as I turn the meter off,

trash the strip and choose a new tract
to stick the insulin in.

The python uncoils from its catch, slinks
beneath a rusty harrow.

The woman weaves marigolds
in her son's wet hair,

climbs beside him
on the bamboo board.

The current ferries them off the canvas, stretched
over blue tile. Marigolds

spill into my hamper, crimson petals
on the bathroom floor.

Advice for Pallbearers

To make the sound of your footsteps
disappear requires practice,

a cornfield in late autumn
when the ground is brittle enough

to repeat what it hears.
Best if the six of you can go together

at dusk, find a barn-owl,
a corn-crow will do.

See how close you can get
before the bird startles,

observe the interaction
of air and wing.

Before you handle the casket,
borrow your mother's finest crystal

vase, carry it through the crowded parking lot
to the water park, ride the slides.

Let nothing shatter.
The trick is for the coffin to appear

to float, the weight of his failures
superfluous. Let him be known

as a saint, for a few moments,
before he is forgotten.

King Tide

Down, in the unadorned darkness
of the Twin Peaks tunnel,
you pretended not to know me.

You'd sit a few rows up on the train ride
home from school, the skin around the barbell
in the nape of your neck

inflamed. Back then,
I didn't understand that details
made life worth living—

I had no need to tell a crow
from a raven, rock candy
from clear pellets of meth,

I never thought to tell anyone
about the black stains scored
on your boyfriend's teeth.

*

Today, the conductor sounds the bell
and the streetcar emerges
into the city's western quarter.

The homeless don't come
to this part of San Francisco
often, owing as much

to the temperament
of the affluent as to the viscous fog
which blots the awnings

on West Portal avenue the same way it did
the year Brian Cotter, sixteen,
pissed on malt liquor and desperate

to prove his straightness took the dare
to dash across the tracks,
which shivered as the train approached.

*

Along this route, every corner is alive
with memory. On Taraval street,
crows leap between wires

and the blue-tiled bell tower
of St. Cecilia's comes into view.
They held Brian's service there.

Father O'Shea must have looked
towards that tower in the evening
after fondling children in the belfry.

*

We never went to mass
but I played on the church's teams.
The shortstop's father was the only neighbor

mom knew by name. The others we referred to
by their jobs and the flaws of their gardens. There was the judge
with the over-pruned cypress, the surgeon

with the parched peonies and the rhododendron
that refused to bloom. This was the city
but it was prim as the suburbs,

and I knew you lived for the glares
they cast at your blue hair, the Sex Pistols patches
and the spikes studded in your jeans.

*

When I get off the train at 46th, I take the short cut
to the highest dunes at Ocean Beach.
The red blaze of ice-plant yields

to the corduroy of swell lines, cormorants
hunting mackerel, which swirl a single ring
beneath the building waves.

Then I walk the beach along the retaining wall
where, the year after Brian died, we scrawled
his name in black Krylon

(framed by a crooked wreath
of Celtic crosses, four leaf clovers),
then his name again in red marker

(above a drawing of his corpse, prostrate,
covered by a sheet, his feet protruding from the fabric.)
It was six years after we buried Brian

that you drowned in your vomit,
and I, twenty-two, and thrust, again,
into death's rituals, would read

that the Sumerians covered their corpses
in shrouds, but left the feet uncovered
so that the souls could find their way West—

*

Where the train line ends.
West, where the foghorns and the tugboats
usher tankers into Oakland, and the cranes start

the big rigs on their diesel creep
towards the strip malls.
Your coroner's report read *Suicide*

due to the sea of drugs
in your system. All those years
of self-sabotage and diabetes,

failed attempts and hospital stays. You should know
mom lobbied to have the record changed.
She was doing so much better,

she told the man who held your file,
she didn't want to die.
West, where on a clear day,

we saw, together, the Farralons heave
like the haunches of a dragon.
Today the islands are hidden

by a fog so dense it seems to leaven.
I taste the sacrament as I arrive
at the water and slip off my jeans.

Prayer for the Instant City

In the makeshift mosque,
twenty-four men kneel,
heads pressed to the straw carpet.
In white linen, khaki slacks,
they bend like egrets in the shallows,
talking God's love,
that sweet, rasping toad.

Look at the marks on their foreheads,
Hasan tells me, as we begin
our shift. You can see who prays the most.
We are delivering tents
for the hundreds that arrive
from Homs, Aleppo,
the villages between.
A camp becomes a city
the way a wound
becomes a scar.

Beside their fathers,
the smallest boys pray.
I have never seen my father bow
but once in the woods
after my sister's death
he called the ground up to him.
Eyes closed, leaning into filtered light,
the leaves and the soil
came, the ants crawled
across his prayer.

The Arabic script tilts, each hymn
a calligraphy of ships
the imam steers,
his voice like water
slapping the hull, a call

plaited voices answer—
by *You we enter the evening,*
by *You we enter the morning.*
The ship's wake widens
into silence.

When we were children,
my sister buried my father
to the neck in sand.
He smiled as her yellow pail
emptied on his chest.
I placed a chipped
white limpet over each
of his eyes.

I Ask My Sister's Ghost How Dying Is

And she weighs the oath of secrecy the dead take
against the pact we made in the crawl space

beneath the front porch, our birthmarks
pressed together, her cheek against my wrist.

It's like gathering dolls from the debris
of the great Pacific plastic patch,

filling your dinghy with their pale figures,
lying down among them the way we hid

in tupelo. Like one doll taking your hand
and you realize she's lost two fingers

as the boat drifts beyond the plastic
and the stars begin to boil

in the navy sky. Like knowing the story
of every constellation is wrong,

trying to tell the dolls Orion is a butterfly mistaken
for a warrior when they begin to sing the magnificat

in chorus and place a thousand hands
on your body, tug your eyelids into position.

Two by two they turn, making no splash
as they leave you to the sound of laughter,

mixing with the brine. Her voice quiets.
I realize my eyes are closed

when I open them and find myself
alone in dim light beneath my father's porch,

the wind slipping through slats,
something scratching in the corner.

Spill

I follow my father down a corridor
of laurel. Where I see wild,
he sees symmetry—
red trillium
refutes winter's theorem,
distant ridges divide place
into watershed,
basin.

I don't understand this mathematics
he makes of the world,
but I follow close
in case he speaks,
tasting yarrow, sorrel,
when he picks it.

The trail opens at the tainted river.
When the samples are capped,
levels tallied in a ledger
no one will see,
he rolls up the sleeve of my sweater.

His finger traces the path
of the spill's damage,
or is he reading my palm?
Naming the crease
where the heart-line fuses
with the head.

I know not to ask what might come,
cup my hand
as if guarding a damselfly.

The Hermitage at Laurel Dell

Of a life playing Bach for moss
on a swollen cello,

lying for days
in a field of milkmaids,

undressing in fog to translate Jeffers—
wolle, entfernung, stein, Wahrheit,

only six rotted railroad ties remain
and a few microfiche slides

of Emil Barth's meticulous cursive
filling the page— *A buck,*

plus what's foraged, feeds you well enough,
he wrote in his journal,

March eight, nineteen sixteen,
but a boar, salted and cured, is divine.

When the poets came to visit,
he didn't tell them he was unhappy,

nearly always sick.
He toasted with plum mead,

laughed at stories of their trysts.
So what, touch haunts you,

he told himself when they'd gone,
drinking from the spring,

scrubbing his doubt with clear water,
the bombs would fall, anyway.

Halo for the Scorched Orchard

in the pause between death and tendril the farmer kneels where the gage tree grew knowing she will stay

I Ask My Sister's Ghost How Her Days Are Now

Do you remember those picture books
where the illustrator removes the outer wall

of a jumbo jet to show children where luggage goes,
how the pilots' levers connect to wings?

Where diagrams reveal the way smoke escapes
through stacks in a sugar factory,

the four hundred yellow-tipped
missiles a warship's hull can hold?

And how on most pages
you could find a bathroom in the schema,

and a nail-sized man with blue pants around his ankles
reading the paper while quietly shitting?

I feel just like that man now.
Doing my business, everyone oblivious

to my presence, and if by chance they see me,
they chuckle, as if my lone role is to make light

of the pain on the pilot's face,
the underpaid laborers threshing cane,

the marines playing ping-pong
as the turrets open

and we rain down hellfire on the next village
where the word for beauty

sounds just like the word for camel, and the phrase
I borrowed sometimes means I burned.

Masa

I thought my sister's ashes
would feel like masa.
Clumpy, maybe, but milled
free from her figure.

But when I cup a handful
to sow in the canyon
where we gathered nasturtiums,
I meet flame's laziness—

two triangles of bone
intact among the powder—
a vertebrae's corner?
Her middle phalanx

that steadied the blade
she pulled across her wrist?
Arrowheads
we should have left

in the cornfield, cobalt
glass the sea spit up,
or the sails of the toy ship
we captained in the tub,

water sloshing over the porcelain rim
as we summoned a squall
through which only fools
like us would sail.

2.

Rendering the Pose

I.

After sketching figures, a student rolls up his pant leg
and recounts the accident—Guatemala, the mountain road
where two buses collided in a flash of yellow fury.
My rodilla was aquí, he said, pointing left,
pero my foot was ahí, pointing right, *dangling.*

I picture the buckled buses, cracked windshields
declaring the names of the drivers' lovers
in bright, beveled letters—Lupita, Esmeralda,
one of whom became a widow as traffic backed up
and people left their idling cars
to watch the injured file out carrying the dead.

I'm not sure how he learned that word,
dangling, before the word knee,
but I admire that he used it just the same.
Don't worry mister, he said, turning to leave,
we die seven times before to stop breathing.

II.

If death comes seven times, then my first death
was in realizing the smallness of my life.
That my students' blemished faces
are the only ones my life will touch.
That my paintings will gather in basements,
bargain aisles. That the scent of eucalyptus
drifting through the window in August
will form my strongest memory of this city,
the only city I will call home and mean it.

A strange kind of death, that first dying—
I look toward the vastness of the landscape.
The sea always walking away from the horizon.

III.

Last week, during a self-portrait exercise,
the student drew himself as a fish
snared on a hook. How spare
his marks on the page—
the single inked stroke of the pole,
arc of the fishing line, sharp curve of the barb piercing
the fish's mouth, the seething scrawls
implying the surface of water.
Who is the fisherman here? I asked.
His eyes settled on his hands.

IV.

Naming pain is a kind of violence.
A terrible art best done with gesture, allegory.
So that when I say *time hunts with its baited hook,*
I should flash my hand like a lure, for effect.

Or when I say *all day in the eucalyptus grove*
I confess myself to starlings, I mean my human heart
is starving for forgiveness.

And when I answer the phone
and that student stammers on the line,
my uncle locked the door again, he won't let me in,
and I reply, *I'll pick you up, be ready in an hour—*

what I want to say is, *there is a tradition in pottery*
where shards are melted down, then pounded again
to form a stronger clay.

I want to say, *can I show you the picture I drew of myself*
when I was your age? It was like yours. In pencil,
I made myself a spider hanging from thread,
my eight legs flailing.

V.

I scoured my room to find the drawing.
In a shoebox full of cowries, slap bracelets, warped pastels—
the last photograph of my family together.
My mother in her favorite dress, my face
against the blue linen. My sister, five years old,
stroking my hair, singing as my mother hummed—
I forget the words but not the tune,
not the scent of buckwheat boiling on the stove,
my father's beard like kelp when he kissed us
into barnacle dreams. Not the rhythm
of my mother's rocking. The map she traced on my back—
her fingers circling my birthmark, that dark sun
setting in the lake of my body.

VI.

At last I found the drawing, the lines faded,
the image now the mark a rock makes
when hurled through a window.
What cliché would I use to explain this to the student?
The window is the holy family, I am the rock, we all need rebellion.
Or maybe, I am the stained-glass window, the sun glows in my orange body,
the crack is where I have sinned, you have to do right.

Instead, I chose another sketch called Horse and Rider,
where the rider is the self and the horse is life
and I am the towhee they are riding past. I am preening.
Even then I loved to watch life gallop past me.
Just look at the rider pull back on the reins
when she moves beneath my branch.
Just watch her lie beneath my tree, unmoving.

VII.

When I arrived at the student's house he was shivering,
the cold of the stoop in his bones.
We drove to the city pier. I had a thermos of soup
that burned his tongue, I had a fishing pole but no bait.
We cast the line anyway. Crabs congregated on the stones
beneath our swinging legs, the bay a stained-glass window
in morning's cathedral, sun rays hexing ripples,
sending the seagulls into a hysterics of salt.

The line tugged and I knew we were saved.
But we reeled in a roper-toed boot,
kelp caught in the grommets.
No banished warrior hid inside
waiting to emerge, no lore, no legend.
Who is the fisherman here?
he mimicked, knocking the boot back to the bay.

VIII.

The word care has roots in the Gothic kara—
to cry out with, to lament. If it is an act of solidarity,
my role was merely to witness his sorrow.
Even that degree of tenderness makes men
uncomfortable.

As he slipped into the alley behind his apartment,
I parked my car to find a diner
and thought, I have been so alone in my pain.

In each shop, the language changed—
strawberries, fresas, caomei.
After the markets, split-levels,
every fifth house abandoned, the lemon trees overflowing
with neglect, fruit spoiling out of reach.

Outside the Grace Baptist, a creaking real estate sign:
Open House for Souls.
The vestibule was empty.
It had been years since I'd entered a church
but the nave smelled the same.

I sat in a pew with my sketchbook.
How my hand delighted tracing the bannister's curves,
the crosses scored in the candelabra, the vase of blood
lilies on the altar.

I rendered the lead cames in the windows—
their cross-hatched texture,
a Jacob's ladder streamed through

I always misrepresent the light—
draw it pouring
when it spills, dancing
when stillness brims
inside my chest.

The pastor sat beside me, watching the page fill.
A charcoal arch

     Not bad...

above the slatted grate
of the confessional booth,

     Not bad at all...

the dark hole
I could never bring myself
to speak through.

IX.

Another death is the death of memory.
But only some memories wither.
It's Darwinian, what remains becomes the standard
against which life is measured—

Grace:

My father's hands
on my sister's corpse,
removing the ring
from her septum,
sliding it on his pinky,
brushing her bleached
bangs into place.

Grief:

Time slowing down,
its white sail luffing
against turquoise water.
Time diving from its yacht,
peering through a mask
at pillars of spawning coral.
Time indifferent
to your mourning.
Time do you hear me?
They all say—
just give it time.
Time dropping its anchor,
time in the dingy.
No matter the size of the waves,
time always
reaches the shore
of its chosen island,
orders a margarita.

X.

This is what the student remembered of the crash:
A basket of eggs flung from the farmer's lap
in the bus seat beside him. The eggs in the air—
ellipses fixed, for an instant,
an hour?

The images memory chooses
have nothing to do with us.

He crawled through twisted metal
past the nun with shards in her arm,
past the newly dead—
In my dreams their open eyes . . . azulito—

little blue,
pale blue that hides
in grey,
speckled blue
abandoned in a nest
two days before hatching,
Marian blue
of the virgin's robes—
how she blushes in her portrait
on the tattered card
tucked in his wallet,
blush of vigor, blush
of shame, blush of sky
swilling the sun's blessing
bestowed to all,
even the farmer bled out
on the mountain road
as the engine caught fire,
even his brooding hens,
no one left to feed them.

XI.

The seven deaths need not be chronological.
There are ghosts who have died in body
(the seventh death), but retain perfect recollection of their lives.

Unable to create new experiences, their memory sharpens.
These are the ghosts to worry about.
They plant seeds of doubt in certainty, they whisper
in your ear as you sleep, forecasting the next day.

My mother says my father had a ghost like this.
I saw it once sulking in the corner
wearing a frayed, gray blazer,
rolling a cigarette and speaking of a better life,
prodding him to leave us.

XII.

When I returned from the church, my room was as I left it—
boxes open, my mother watching me from photographs
strewn on the floor, her wrinkles bending toward the years.

Lately she has been resisting the death
of the part of the heart that loves
unconditionally.

Only her plants keep it alive, people having failed her.
Transaction is simpler in this kingdom;
water for bloom, pare in November, for fruit come June.

She walks among trained azaleas,
past the monkey flowers,
the passion vine, its oval lobes woven
through the trellis, fiddleheads bursting yellow
song, the swing dance of peas climbing string.

If I die early, if there is agency in reincarnation,
I will come back a snail, I will inch out
into my mother's sorrel and munch the broad greens
with ten thousand teeth.

In the morning, when she puts her fingers
around the whorl of my shell, lowers me into the pail,
I will have meant something,
I will have marked my way back to that garden.

XIII.

At dusk, I put on the frayed, gray blazer
and stand in my concrete yard
watching gingko leaves pirouette into winter.

Lives fall away less elegantly—
each time, like a boot kicked from a pier,
finding home beside the tires full of sludge the snipe eels nest in.

In the middle of the night, the eels emerge, their teeth
glinting in the deep, while up above, my phone glows twice:

Mister they say I can't come back
I have nowhere to go.

I imagine him walking up International
as midnight's patients arrive to their neon convalescence.
Finding the park benches occupied, he walks on
to the church, the only door unlocked.

The nave gaping now, every footstep
echoing in the aisle, every breath held
as if a ceremony were set to begin.
He lies down on a pew,
takes the knife from his pocket, guides the blade
through lacquer, carving lines in the grain.

Two lines meeting in opposing directions
give an impression of severity,
or even violence; I read as his class practiced still lifes—

a backlit bowl of eggs beside an empty blue bottle—

If a third line is added,
the opposition is softened
an effect of unity and completeness produced.

XIV.

I want to write the student, to comfort him.
But I'm kinder to the dead than I am to the living.
So I write to the farmer, to the ghost
who haunts my father, and to my younger self
who shaved the speedball with a razor,
white rock whittled into three snowy ridges.

I didn't hand my sister the coiled bill,
but I didn't stop her
the last time she said, *again.*

I crumple the drafts.
My hand insists—
again, my sister's name:

    Dear Rebecca,

    Whichever words spell out forgiveness
    are meant to be sung, not spoken.
    If I hum the melody, will you sing along?

The black ink dangling between perforated lines.
A phone wire swings in the night wind,
the waxing moon glances off the bay.

I lean into the shining,
knowing there can be no unity, no completeness,
no finality of vision. Just lines attempting order

and failing, shapes weighted and arranged,
the empty white space holding them apart.

Still, I trace my sister's face on the page.
Her eyes open, gaze settling just beyond me
the way it always did— as if watching a mare
gallop through a crater.

Maybe she can hear me over the hooves
thudding on the crust.

3.

Hunting Chanterelles in the Oakland Hills

It is not only trauma which cleaves—
the soul also fractures in joy.

All month I summon the shard of myself
still kneeling in the sword-fern,

tracing the forked ridges of winter's first chanterelle,
but it won't leave the scent—

soil pinched with pepper, apricot,
to return to the city,

where another piece of me mutters
under the overpass, looking for a fix.

Sometimes when I plead
for my fragments to join,

I hear my mother's voice,
calling her dead daughter home.

Slow down, my friend insists,
off-trail in deep woods,

they're easy to miss.
Rain spills from my cap

as I scour the chaparral,
bending to buckeye roots,

digging through duff. *There*,
flesh worthy of the name, *chanterelle*.

I remove the veil of mud
as if it were lace,

I splinter when my fingers slip
the stem from loam.

The Rungs

Only the person with the green dice should be talking,
I remind the boys, holding up the oversized foam cubes.

And the others should be? Listening, K. says,
and how should we listen? Con el corazón, M. replies,

thumping his chest with his closed fist.
That's right, I say, with the heart. Who wants to start?

The dice are passed around the circle
and the boys gloss over the check-in question.

When they reach B., who walked here, unaccompanied,
from Honduras three months ago, he holds them like boulders.

We straighten when his lip begins to quiver.
It's not my place to tell you what he shared that day.

But I can tell you how M. put his hand on B.'s back
and said, maje, desahógarte,

which translates roughly to un-drown yourself,
though no English phrase so willingly accepts

that everyone has drowned, and that we can reverse that gasping,
expel the fluids from our lungs.

I sit quietly as the boys make, with their bodies, the rungs of a ladder,
and B. climbs up from the current, sits in the sun

for a few good minutes before he jumps back in.
The dice finish the round and we are well over time.

I resist the urge to speak about rafts, what it means to float.
Good, I tell them, let's go back to class.

After handshakes and side hugs, I'm left alone in the small room
with a box of unopened tissues, two starburst wrappers on the ground.

Futile, — the winds —

I.

My sister once told me that when it gets hot enough in Arizona,
and it always does this time of year,
the wayward pelicans, lost on their migration north,
see steam rising from the desert road
and confuse it for the surface of water.
Seeking refuge from the heat,
they plunge into the mirage.
The concrete receives them,
snaps their bones.

II.

When we were children, she placed gifts beneath a stone
on the porch while I slept—urchin spines,
sand dollars; sometimes, she cracked open the discs,
arranged the shards in an arrow.

III.

Among the rocks below the cliffs, between two boulders
sharp with mussels, clinging, the corpse of a brown pelican.
The keel bone juts through the slumped flesh,
the skull bows to the sea. I kneel,
its bill turns to powder in my hand.
I, too, want to die enormous in a tide pool.

IV.

Did she forget our cypress on the bluff?
We climbed so high just to lie on branches, our hands
almost touching beneath the curtain of sky,
the runs in the blue fabric like so many roads
the birds traverse, their flight stitching the folds
like the sutures the doctor sewed into her wrists.

How creaky, those branches,
and the crows, cawing.

V.

Dusk, I pitch camp above the tideline.
When my sister plunged, and the winds did nothing,
did she know the song bones sing
just before they snap? I hum that slow song.
My heart a thousand wilted feathers.
I pluck one, press the tip into the sand.
My breath eddies through the plume.

and leaves a cardboard box on my porch. I place the parcel on my table and consider whether to open it or call my mother, whose hip is giving out. Inside the delivered box, another package with the same rectangular dimensions, the same sky-blue tape sealing the slits. Did I order something? Neither box has a label. Inside the second package, a third, slightly smaller. I think of nested silver spoons, a set of Russian dolls—the chain of dark-eyed daisies intricately painted on a scarf tied around the plump matriarch's face as she returns from threshing wheat in a distant field somewhere, a black hen beneath her arm. But this is no parable of winter. Inside the third box, styrofoam peanuts surround a dozen chocolate globes the size of marbles. I pick one up and cradle the map printed on the wrapper—the world rendered borderless, a land mass contiguous and beige. Someone told me if you inflate a marble to the size of the Earth the imperfections on the seemingly smooth glass would form unclimbable mountains, plumbless seas. I shed the foil from the small Earth and crumple the wrapper into a silver moon and place the milk-chocolate mantle beneath my tongue, lie down among the cardboard and styrofoam, and feel the plates shift and the crust buckle inside my body, where demand for connection always outpaces supply.

Lines for John Berryman on the Bus from Little Mogadishu

You jumped from the bridge a few blocks from here,
        onto the west bank of the Mississippi.

It was a Friday morning in January,
        icicles must have jeweled the trusses—
how bright they shine today.

But I'm not writing to describe the city.
I need to ask what it takes to point your toes
        and slice through mantle,

        to crawl around the groans
          of a winter flume.

John, this is not despair, not even boredom—

        but the grind of air brakes, Drake crooning
        through my neighbor's earbuds, a diesel engine
        down Washington Avenue,

        they all mask stone's tectonic lust.

Should I confess, I was happy once?

        Ten months chasing weasels from olive groves
          in Liguria.

        Do fields in the afterlife need tending,
          too?

I think of you in that sunken garden, shears
        in your pocket,

as you pour a shot into your coffee
        and watch bees weave

in and out of the buckbrush,
       lingering on the broad
    whiskey petals of your breath.

Salve Regina

They thumbed up from Santa Ana that morning
for a job with the Catholic Worker smearing mustard
under pastrami, stacking iceberg on Dutch crunch,
passing sandwiches and seltzer to the residents
of the third largest encampment beneath the Eight-Eighty.
Rufo was more handsome. But it was Faustine
whose voice most effortlessly dwelled in the 15th century basilica
their singing built in the middle of the room,
when, after an hour of receptive silence, they sat back to back
chanting ecclesiastic Latin: O clemens, O pia,
O dulcis Virgo Maria. What did I know? I was merely one of many
confusing Marx with Hegel gathered that night
to hear a Sioux elder share news from Standing Rock
at the canticle farm in East Oakland, which
that time of year was ringed by lemon trees
bursting into yellow prayer. Come morning,
Rufo and I would pack citrus in three wicker baskets
for the elder to drive back across the plains.
As I pressed my nose to rind, Rufo told me
how each morning his father dusted chili on sliced lemon,
how anything could be a sacrament if you held it right.

The Arachnologist

When he told me his teeth felt too heavy
to study history, I excused him.
I knew he was headed for the aqueduct,

or the boarded-up houses choked
by trumpet vine where he found them.
Martel collected spiders with the discipline of a surgeon.

He kept them in empty soda bottles
under his bed. On his way into sixth period,
he touched my fist with his fist,

announced the genus of his catch,
Latrodectus, and his total, *that's nine this week!*
Through this tally of arachnids captured

in sugary plastic, we learned to trust each other
the way men on tankers far out at sea
confide reluctantly in gray rippling water.

When his best friend broke the news,
they found Martel last night, her voice quavering,
stray bullet off International,

I went to his house to adopt a spider.
I imagined the red hourglass
on the female's abdomen emptying itself

slowly, her segmented body imprisoned
in the glow of the green-tinted bottle,
but no one was home. Now when I hear

the old women gathering cans at dawn,
half-swallowed by blue waste bins,
I think of Martel finding containers

to bring to the canyon, Martel
inspecting stones, placing his fingers
delicately around the thorax,

the eight legs angry at the morning
as he lifts the orb weaver to the sun,
offering what he loved to the old, hungry light.

The Last Bear in the Headlands

I case the marina for three months until
I declare the sloop abandoned. It's
perfect, I tell you, and since our rent
has doubled, what choice do we have
but to make it perfect?

We seal the leaks
and buff the rust, the empties left in the
cabin make enough at the aluminum
exchange for a few weeks' worth of
lentils. At evening, you paint the city's
changing skyline in your muted palate
and I walk through the wetlands
bisected by the freeway.

You never paint
the Golden Gate and I love you for it,
love the way you refuse what is
commonly loved, refuse even the word
love.

The egret's steps stir petrol rings
and I count the slick, concentric ripples
as if tallying years on a slab of wood,
noting the dry decades where the rings
tighten followed by thick bands of
plenty, billows of fog, rain sheets
filtering through roots which don't go
deep, but wide.

Most days I go swimming
before you wake even though the bay
is sick, the bull kelp bobs and the
mussels lining the pier at low tide are
the color of a bruise, and what is a
bruise but the body fighting back? I

crawl in the cot beside you smelling of neoprene, the boat lolling in the hum of I-80. Your paintings hang on every inch of the cabin and through the circular window the brown grasses of the headlands sway across the bay, a light rain etching the space between cloud and land.

I want to wake you and tell you the hill is like the pelt of a bear, the rain its tongue, that the last bear in the headlands is the headlands itself, but I know you will turn the simile against the modes of production. The clouds work east across the bay, the tongue matting the bear's fur until it looks like it has emerged from fishing for the salmon it hopes will return to Tamalpais creek, any day now they'll come, and I kiss you while you sleep but not in an obvious way.

Steam rises from white tea as you mix a can of paint with one chopstick, acrylic flecks slip on the floor beside you and why bother cleaning them, you always say, why not give the constellation a name, a moon, a mythology. I wonder what you will paint us into as the streetlights shine down on the tent city across I-80, the rain letting up and the clouds parting, the night swelling with AM radio and umbrage as Saturn's rings slip out of focus in the telescope I found by the tracks and swore I'd finally fixed.

Sonora Desert Halo

from the ironwood to the thermal to the slow descending circles the vulture draws around the lost boy's body and back

I Ask My Sister's Ghost to Take Me with Her

Not because the reefs are bleaching.
Because I want to see how thin the veil is.

To row behind her in the boat
she came in, row all day

into night and where the river turns
to delta, blade my oar to beach the dingy

on a bank of silt and cattail.
Because I want to hide with her

in midnight's swaying, turn my ears
from the throng of bullfrogs

to the song she hums,
listen to her stories of its blind composer,

how he charmed wives at the Royal parties
in Dublin, his fingers sweeping

each glissando, his eyes clouded over
like a cod on ice.

There is a Chinese symbol she taught me for a word
that has no word, but I can never remember

how to draw it, what tone
to put in my throat to speak.

The inked shape of that mutable mark hangs
just beyond the last branch of my mind

as she turns to leave.
There is nothing I can say

to convince her to take me,
so I pluck the tongue from my mouth

and lay it flat on a stone.
When she bends to inspect

the petal, it becomes a red door.
It creaks as she opens it,

walks into the unspoken
without turning back.

4.

I Ask My Sister's Ghost to Play a Game of Cribbage

I set up the good board with the mahogany pegs,
warm the bourbon and stir in cider.

We sit between woven peacocks on the Persian rug,
the cards blur and plume as I shuffle them.

You want to know about sex in the afterlife?
We've never spoken of the body, or its pleasures,

and I don't want to speak of them now.
It's better than poetry, she tells me anyway,

but worse than cheap whiskey.
Better than addiction, but worse than denial.

She completes the crib and we begin the count.
In a peacock's beak, a sprig of wheat shakes in braided wind.

Better than a royal flush, she smiles, laying her cards between us
but nothing like shooting the moon.

As she moves her pegs up the board I can't help picturing the mechanics
of making love without the body—

maybe the slow deliverance of shadows fusing in a field
at dusk. Or is it more abstract?

There are times I've merged without touching.
When I lie down in the meadow where we spread your ashes,

the world seeps into me, I tell her,
unfurls a vine around my throat.

She lowers her cards, picks at the carpet's warp.
Well, she asks, *do you like it?*

Like what? I answer, my cheeks red with shame.
That pressure. Death's breath on your neck.

And though the grip nearly splits me,
I realize, for the first time, that I do.

Little Accents

Kandinsky, as the war raged on,
turned away from severity
towards a brighter palette.

The lavishness of purple
as Warsaw was reduced to rubble.

Not *stubborn, just greedy,*
Jack Gilbert said
of his self-imposed exile on Monolithos.

I envy his poems, their pitchers
of Greek honey.

Some poets move to barren islands
just to drop stones
down old wells, just to revel in the sound
that rises after.

We despise in others
what we are ashamed of
in ourselves—

Koalas, on fire,

the biblical spread of the virus,

and me paddling out at the point break
practicing trimeter—

Little accents, wild
iris under redwood
in the rain, I kneel to touch
the brushwork.

The Kaleidoscope

Things got dark for David Brewster
after inventing the kaleidoscope.
For his last fifty years, people only asked
about his simplest invention.
Kalos—beauty, Eidos—form, Skopios—view,
he'd explain to each new member
of the Royal Society, sighing
as their learned eyes streaked grease
on the double lens.

My teacher said that even after his comrades were slaughtered,
people mostly asked him to read the love sonnets
he'd written in his twenties.

Even this poem.
All this poem really wants
is to make love again in Valparaíso,
to praise my lover's eyes
with the word *crepúsculo*— twilight,
then lie down,
twist the brass knob
and watch the world and all its sadness swirl
into tinted red triangles,
refracted blue spheres bursting
into a future where the generals
bear no mention.

Braille in Sicily

My Grandfather, legally blind, in the fig orchard.
The bumps on the ripe skin
like the small beads at the point of each diamond
on his lover's fishnet stockings.
Every Thursday for twenty-three years,
he slipped the briar as his family slept,
hurried down the backroad to Agrigento, up
spiral stairs to the harlequin's room.

My Grandmother shares this as she washes
parsley, her ring glinting in the faucet's stream.
It's not wrong to call a diamond a rhombus—
meaning, in Greek, something that spins.
Through the kitchen window, we watch him sway
at the orchard's edge, a fig between his teeth.
He thinks I don't know, she says, *it's better that way.*
I'm the one with the secrets.

Outside Tallahassee

At the base of a waterfall, a boy
offers to sell me his chameleon
and I ask if I can pay for it in stars.
Mist leaps off the rocks—the night is warm
and the spray emboldens me.
How about those two, the twins,
I say, pointing toward Castor + Pollux
clinking like silver coins in the southern sky.
Make it the Little Dipper, he insists,
so I reach to bend down the Little Dipper
and the three of us pretend to drink
the thin, piquant cosmos. When the ladle empties,
he tucks the constellation in his back pocket
like a slingshot and retreats down the hillside.
In the moon dark, my chameleon's sharp toes
grip my skin as he climbs my limbs,
the astral sheen on his lips gleaming
like the astral sheen on mine.

Halo for Evacuees

the grasses higher and the grasses foment the wilder flame and the flame even the faithless pray for the rain that lures

Self-Portrait with Daughter

Ash whit curling
     in the lilac.

     Frog lips stenciled
on the surgeon's mask

my daughter wears
     to keep out smoke.

     Will the firebreak hold?

Machines raze the fuel load
     six valleys East

     as the wind turns
cedar, and the sirens insist:

     Will the firebreak hold?

The wind turning juniper,
     at dusk.

     After dinner, my daughter
shades red crayon lipstick

above the cake of haze
     on the mask, and I almost forget

the world I have given.

In the morning
     we step out to stare at the sun,

     our shadows thick,
quivering.

Chosen Landscape

Sometimes, the sea plays its green piano
in the 4/4 time of the blues.

Sometimes it plays nocturnes
the moon knows how to glimmer on.

The way the sea hammers the keys, tonight,
if I could take my sister's hand

I'd lead her into the breaking
waves, so we could become the keys

the sea plays, so we could feel a hundred fingers
strum along our eyes.

And if, when the refrain came, my sister asked,
have I heard this song before?

Would I tell her, *it's the song mom sang
as she spread your ashes on the bluff?*

The terns riding slow thermals above us.
Or would I duck beneath the surface?

Wrap myself in ringing water
as if it were the worn blanket

she pressed around me
before turning out the lights,

leaving me to dreams of white birds
hunting in gray water.

The Nest
for Alfredo Espino

This morning
I watched a goldfinch
disappear into a tree
through a hole no bigger

than my open mouth.
From the hollow
the finch
began her crooning.

That's what poetry is
I thought—
not the tree,
but the hidden song.

Not the yellow bird,
but the instinct to climb
inside the darkness
to sing.

I Ask My Sister's Ghost to Write Her Own Elegy

Since the attempts I've made fall short.
She leads me to the creek

where she spent her last years
testing toxins for the state.

The place is nothing special, a slash
between two developments, a twinkie wrapper,

cigarette butts embedded in the bank.
That's how nature in the city is, the allure

emerges only after many visits, flora
noticed by a patient eye—*You're doing it again,*

she interrupts, *describing the land instead of me.*
She points towards the water.

In the shallows a crayfish pretends to be a stone.
Then what should I tell people? I ask.

Most days, she says, she just waded in,
let the crayfish crawl over my feet.

She knew them like she knew lovers' scars,
their cleft claws, their ridged antennae.

When the crayfish population quartered,
she told the council it was the sediment

from their new construction.
Say my death was not an act of violence.

Removing a human mind, a mouth to feed,
she says, *is a kind of generosity.*

I wade up to my knees, I want to feel something
crawl across my feet.

An aluminum lid floats past,
my little raft, my paper lantern.

There is only one dam between us
and the coast. There are the soy fields

and almond groves leeching
nitrous clouds into the river.

I hope there is an entrance
to the cold, thrashing sea.

Acknowledgments

My gratitude to the readers and editors of the following journals in which these poems first appeared:

AGNI: The Invisible Hand Knocks Twice, Outside Tallahassee

Alaska Quarterly Review: The Rungs

Berkeley Poetry Review: Halo for the Scorched Orchard, Halo for Evacuees

CutBank: I Ask My Sister's Ghost How Her Days Are Now

Fourteen Hills: The Last Bear in the Headlands

The Greensboro Review: Lines for John Berryman on the Bus from Little Mogadishu

Harpur Palate: The Hermitage at Laurel Dell

Harvard Review: I Ask My Sister's Ghost to Take Me with Her

Indiana Review: Prayer for the Instant City

Iron Horse Literary Review: Rendering the Pose

The Maine Review: Spill

The Mississippi Review: Salve Regina

New Ohio Review: The Arachnologist

Nimrod: Little Accents, I Ask My Sister's Ghost to Write Her Own Elegy

Orion Magazine: The Nest

Poetry East: Hunting Chanterelles in the Oakland Hills

Rappahannock Review: Futile, –the winds–

RHINO Poetry: Masa

Ruminate Magazine: Type Two

Southern Indiana Review: I Ask My Sister's Ghost to Play a Game of Cribbage

Spillway: The Kaleidoscope

Terrain.org: Chosen Landscape

Third Coast: Braille in Sicily, Self Portrait with Daughter

upstreet: Advice for Pallbearers

Washington Square Review: I Ask My Sister's Ghost How Dying Is

Some of these poems were also included in I Ask My Sister's Ghost, a chapbook from DIAGRAM/New Michigan Press (2020). I am grateful to editor Ander Monson for his support and encouragement.

The poem "Type Two" was included in the Best New Poets 2018 Anthology. The poem "I Ask My Sister's Ghost to Take Me with Her" was featured on Poetry Daily. The poem "I Ask My Sister's Ghost to Play a Game of Cribbage" was featured on Verse Daily.

My deepest thanks to Gabrielle Calvocoressi for believing in this work, and to the wonderful team at the University of Utah Press for bringing it into the world.

A special thank you to my dear friend and teacher Ruth Schwartz, who nourished my instinct towards poetry and taught me to find my way towards the heart of the poem. This book would not exist without your guidance. For generous and insightful feedback on this manuscript at various stages of its making, I am grateful to Evan Bissell, Will Brewer, Ryan Bruno, Peter Kline, Brittany Perham and David Roderick. For guidance with individual poems, or for artistic kinship, thank you to Kim Addonizio, Brett Cook, Sarah Crossland, Kyle Hartman, Niko McConnie-Saad, Cintia Santana, Matthew Siegel, John Sibley Williams, Pireeni Sundaralingam, Jennifer Sweeney, Kary Wayson and Noah Warren.

To my parents, Isa & Laura, and Lenny & Connie, I am forever grateful for all that you have taught me, about myself, and about how to keep trying to love the world.

To Lauren, for everything. Without you, cherry blossoms are just cherry blossoms.